G000039812

WOULD YOU RATHER

BOOK FOR ADULTS

by Shut Up Coloring

WOULD YOU RATHER...

make more money
but be busier

make less money
but be less busy?

 or

WOULD YOU RATHER GET YOUR PAYCHECK...

daily

monthly?

 or

WOULD YOU RATHER SLEEP WITH...

your door open   your door closed?

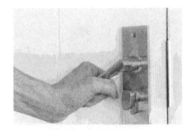   or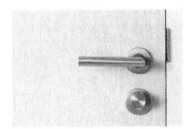

WOULD YOU RATHER ONLY LISTEN TO...

old school music   music from today?

   or

WOULD YOU RATHER...

explore the sea   explore outer space?

   or

WOULD YOU RATHER...

work for yourself   work at
from home   a professional establishment?

   or

WOULD YOU RATHER HAVE...

an amazing cook

an amazing chef?

or

WOULD YOU RATHER BE...

on a reality TV show

on a game show?

or

WOULD YOU RATHER...

travel by road   travel by air?

 or

WOULD YOU RATHER...

do online dating   go on a blind date?

 or

WOULD YOU RATHER...

live somewhere really hot   live somewhere really cold?

   or

WOULD YOU RATHER HAVE...

a lot of acquaintances   just one really close friend?

   or

WOULD YOU RATHER...

dress corporate   dress casual?

   or

WOULD YOU RATHER LIVE IN...

a bubbly neighborhood   a quiet neighborhood?

   or

WOULD YOU RATHER...

own a penthouse   rent a mansion?

 or

WOULD YOU RATHER WATCH...

a thriller movie   a romance movie?

 or

WOULD YOU RATHER...

eat a home-cooked meal   eat take-out?

   or

WOULD YOU RATHER...

go to a gym   work out from home?

   or

WOULD YOU RATHER...

go to a public library   have a library at home?

   or

WOULD YOU RATHER GO WATCH...

a live stage play   a live musical concert?

   or

WOULD YOU RATHER...

give up on junk food   give up on sugary drinks?

or

WOULD YOU RATHER...

look much younger   look much older
than your age   than your age?

or

WOULD YOU RATHER HAVE...

a really loud voice   a really tiny voice?

 or

WOULD YOU RATHER...

pause life right now   fast forward to the future?

 or

WOULD YOU RATHER HAVE...

a really hot shower   a really cold shower?

   or

WOULD YOU RATHER SPEND THE WEEKEND...

indoors   outdoors?

   or

WOULD YOU RATHER HAVE...

celebrity parents   a celebrity lover?

   or

WOULD YOU RATHER...

plan a party   attend a party?

   or

WOULD YOU RATHER...

win gift cards   win cash?

   or

WOULD YOU RATHER...

drink vodka   drink beer?

   or

WOULD YOU RATHER EAT...

something fried   something grilled?

   or

WOULD YOU RATHER...

eat only vegetables   eat only fruits
for a month   for a month?

   or

WOULD YOU RATHER...

buy an expensive car   be gifted with a cheap car?

   or

WOULD YOU RATHER...

go out to eat   have food delivered
to your place?

   or

WOULD YOU RATHER...

stuff yourself with food all day   go the entire day without eating?

or

WOULD YOU RATHER...

be obese   really skinny?

or

WOULD YOU RATHER GO TO...

a wine tasting event   a food tasting event?

   or

WOULD YOU RATHER...

a board game   play a game
                                on your smartphone?

   or

WOULD YOU RATHER...

dye your hair   curl your hair?

   or

WOULD YOU RATHER DRINK...

black coffee   sweetened coffee?

   or

WOULD YOU RATHER GO ON A DATE WITH...

someone with a bright smile   someone with an infectious smile?

or

WOULD YOU RATHER...

be able to sleep   be completely rested
for long hours   after three hours of sleep?

or

WOULD YOU RATHER GO A YEAR...

without watching movies   without watching the news?

   or

WOULD YOU RATHER GET...

a house with lots of spac   a house with a great view?

   or

WOULD YOU RATHER...

cut down on
your sugar intake

cut down on
your salt intake?

or

WOULD YOU RATHER LOOK AFTER...

a friend's child for the weekend

a friend's pet?

or

WOULD YOU RATHER HAVE...

an indoor swimming pool   an outdoor swimming pool?

or

WOULD YOU RATHER HAVE...

a really healthy body   a really attractive body?

or

WOULD YOU RATHER READ...

a fiction book   a nonfiction book?

   or

WOULD YOU RATHER...

be a millionaire   marry a billionaire?

   or

WOULD YOU RATHER YOUR HAIR...

stopped growing   started to grow twice as fast?

   or   

WOULD YOU RATHER DATE...

a doctor   a scientist?

   or   

WOULD YOU RATHER...

live with friends   live alone?

or

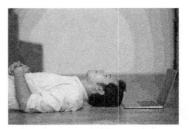

WOULD YOU RATHER TAKE...

a bubble bath   a steamy shower?

or

WOULD YOU RATHER...

do karaoke   watch karaoke performances?

or

WOULD YOU RATHER TAKE A STROLL...

early in the morning   late at night?

or

WOULD YOU RATHER SPEND MONEY ON...

new clothes

new shoes?

or

WOULD YOU RATHER YOUR DAUGHTER...

had no friends

had too many friends?

or

WOULD YOU RATHER...

take selfies   take pictures?

   or

WOULD YOU RATHER DATE...

someone really slim   someone with a lot of flesh?

   or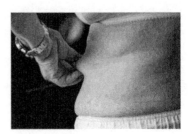

WOULD YOU RATHER TURN UP...

at a wedding   at a birthday party?

   or

WOULD YOU RATHER...

be a kid again   be an elderly already?

   or

WOULD YOU RATHER BE FRIENDS WITH...

an alcoholic   a smoker?

or

WOULD YOU RATHER...

go watch a movie   have friends over
with friends   and watch a movie at home?

or

WOULD YOU RATHER HAVE...

a picnic outside   cook and eat indoors?

 or

WOULD YOU RATHER HAVE A BEST FRIEND...

of the opposite gender   of the same sex?

 or

WOULD YOU RATHER HAVE...

have a pretty girlfriend

have a smart girlfriend?

or

WOULD YOU RATHER...

make a lot
of money at work

get a lot
of vacations from work?

or

WOULD YOU RATHER...

have a chef   be a chef?

   or

WOULD YOU RATHER...

eat fruits   blend and drink fruit juice?

   or

WOULD YOU RATHER DO...

without your phone
for a month

without your laptop
for a month?

or

WOULD YOU RATHER BREAK UP...

by text

by a phone call?

or

WOULD YOU RATHER LIVE...

in the city   in the country?

   or

WOULD YOU RATHER...

visit someone   visit someone
in the hospital   in an elderly home?

   or

WOULD YOU RATHER HAVE...

straight hair   curly hair?

   or

WOULD YOU RATHER...

stop using roll-ons   stop using sprays?

   or

WOULD YOU RATHER DRINK...

hot tea   hot chocolate?

   or

WOULD YOU RATHER BE...

a really fast writer   a really fast reader?

   or

WOULD YOU RATHER...

have wings   have a tail?

   or

WOULD YOU RATHER...

everyone forgot to show up   everyone forgot to show
at your wedding   up to your funeral?

   or

WOULD YOU RATHER...

carry a school-bag to work

wear flip-flops to work?

or
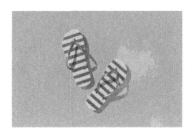

WOULD YOU RATHER...

be in kindergarten again

be in college again?

or

WOULD YOU RATHER HAVE...

really small hands   really large feet?

 or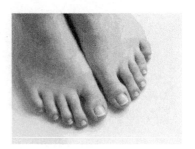

WOULD YOU RATHER...

wear a suit to bed   wear pajamas to work?

 or

WOULD YOU RATHER HAVE...

a third eye   a third ear?

   or

WOULD YOU RATHER...

lock yourself out of   lock yourself out of
your house   your car?

   or

WOULD YOU RATHER...

fall off your chair
at a restaurant

fall off your chair during
a meeting at work?

or

WOULD YOU RATHER...

live with your parents
all your life

have your parents come
around all the time to your place?

or

WOULD YOU RATHER...

sing in the bathroom

sing in front of
a kindergarten class?

or

WOULD YOU RATHER HAVE...

a pet that talks

a carpet that flies?

or

WOULD YOU RATHER BE ALLERGIC...

to hugs

to kisses?

 or

WOULD YOU RATHER HAVE...

eyes that film everything

ears that record everything?

 or

WOULD YOU RATHER HAVE...

a terrible connection
when making calls

terrible connection
when surfing the internet?

or

WOULD YOU RATHER...

eat one thing
for the rest of your life

drink one thing
for the rest of your life?

or

WOULD YOU RATHER...

use glasses   use hearing aids?

 or

WOULD YOU RATHER...

lose your house keys   lose your car keys?

 or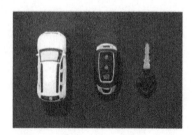

WOULD YOU RATHER...

work at a job you love
and earn pennies

work at a job you hate
and earn a lot?

or

WOULD YOU RATHER...

have your flight delayed

have your flight canceled?

or

WOULD YOU RATHER...

be forced into
an arranged marriage

be single for
the rest of your life?

or

WOULD YOU RATHER BABYSIT...

a child who cries a lot

a child who screams a lot?

or

WOULD YOU RATHER...

take a loan from a bank   borrow money from your parents?

   or

WOULD YOU RATHER HAVE...

an itch that refuses to go   an ache that refuses to go?

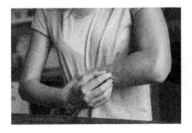   or

WOULD YOU RATHER...

be just friends with
someone you're in love with

get married to
someone you detest?

 or

WOULD YOU RATHER...

get drunk easily

stop drinking alcohol altogether?

 or

WOULD YOU RATHER HAVE TO...

stand all day

sit all day?

or

WOULD YOU RATHER BE...

poor and happy

rich and depressed?

or

WOULD YOU RATHER...

have your car stolen

have your car damaged?

or

WOULD YOU RATHER HAVE TO...

kill a snake

kill a scorpion?

or

WOULD YOU RATHER...

walk in the rain
without an umbrella

walk under the sun
without shades?

or

WOULD YOU RATHER...

twist your ankle

twist your wrist?

or

WOULD YOU RATHER...

bite your tongue accidentally   bite your lips accidentally?

   or

WOULD YOU RATHER DROP YOUR PHONE...

into a bucket of water   into a toilet?

   or

WOULD YOU RATHER HAVE...

your salary slashed
and keep working

resign and be jobless?

or

WOULD YOU RATHER...

fall in love and have
a lot of heartbreaks

never fall in love?

or

WOULD YOU RATHER...

drink something sour   eat something stale?

   or

WOULD YOU RATHER...

eat a bar of soap   suck on a bar of soap?

   or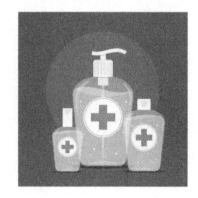

WOULD YOU RATHER...

eat a butterfly

eat a moth?

 or

WOULD YOU RATHER BE PUNCHED...

in the eye

in the nose?

 or

WOULD YOU RATHER MARRY SOMEONE...

who snorts like a pig

who is as dirty as a pig?

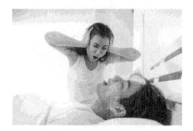

or

WOULD YOU RATHER...

eat raw meat

eat raw fish?

or

Printed in Great Britain
by Amazon

35404068R00036